golf·ing

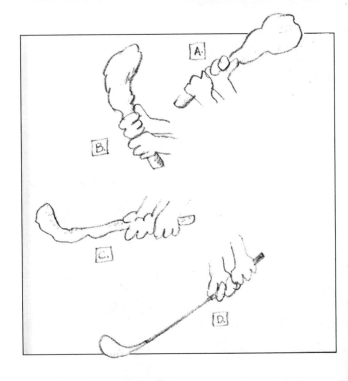

golf·ing
a duffer's dictionary

by Henry Beard
and Roy McKie

Workman Publishing · New York

Library of Congress Cataloging-in-Publication Data

Beard, Henry.
    Golfing: a duffer's dictionary / by Henry Beard and Roy McKie.—Rev.
      p. cm.
ISBN 0-7611-2370-9 (alk. paper)
1. Golf—Dictionaries—Humor.   I. McKie, Roy.   II. Title.

GV967.B38 2001
796.352'03—dc21   00-047747

Workman books are available at special discounts when purchased in bulk for premiums and sales promotions as well as for fund-raising or educational use. Special editions can also be created to specification. For details, contact the Special Sales Director at the address below.

Workman Publishing Company, Inc.
708 Broadway
New York, NY 10003-9555
www.workman.com

Printed in the United States of America

First printing March 2001

10 9 8 7

To those who have heard the call of the tee.

addressing the ball

addressing the ball

Assuming a stance and grounding the clubhead prior to airmailing the ball to a foreign destination. *See* BACKSWING.

advice

As defined by the rules of golf, "any counsel or suggestion made by one golfer to another about the choice of club, method of play, or means of executing a shot, which contains no more than five errors of fact, contradictory statements or harmful recommendations. Six or more such pieces of misinformation or misinstruction shall constitute a formal golf lesson." *See* LESSON TEE.

age players

Accomplished golfers who have recorded either of two exceptional golfing achievements: playing a round of 18 holes at the end of which they had a score identical to their age, or playing a round of 18 holes during all of which they acted their age.

all square A term used in match play to indicate that both teams or individuals have cheated on an equal number of holes. See BEST BALL.

amateur A golfer who is happy if, after paying $125 for greens fees and a cart rental, $50 in the pro shop, and $20 at the halfway house, he ends up winning a $5 Nassau. *See* PROFESSIONAL.

approach shot

A shot which, if it had not caught the lip of the bunker and dropped back into the sand, would have rolled across the green and gone into the water. *See* CHIP SHOT and PITCH.

approach shot

apron Fringe of low grass, or "frog hair," surrounding the green from which golfers usually make an indecisive jabbing stroke combining elements of a chip, a pitch, and a putt that produces a shot known as a "chupp," a "putch," or, simply, "chitt!"

away The player whose ball lies farthest from the hole is "away" and is required by the rules of golf to make the first shot. If, after the stroke is taken, his ball still lies farther from the hole than that of any other member of his playing group, the rules permit him to kick the first bag and throw the first club.

back door

The far side of the cup opposite a player's ball on the green. Sometimes a putt will curve around the cup and enter by this "back door," but more frequently it chooses to wait politely on the "back steps," sit down on the "back porch," or go for a nice long stroll in the "back yard."

back nine The second
9 holes of an 18-hole golf
course, a name derived from
the fact that by the time you
get there, your back aches, your
slice is back, play is backed up,
and your opponent is about
to win all his money back.
See FRONT NINE.

backspin Reverse spin imparted to a golf ball that causes it to "back up" on a green after landing, created by the solid contact of the clubface with the back of the ball or the presence of a bunker, a water hazard, or a steep slope directly below the hole.

backswing

A distinct and pronounced turn of the hips and shoulders that moves the club away from the ball, usually followed by a shot that produces a distinct and pronounced turn of the stomach. See DOWNSWING.

ball

Dimpled, rubber-covered, solid- or composite-cored high-compression sphere with a weight of 1.62 ounces and a diameter of 1.68 inches that will enter a cup 4.25 inches wide and 4.0 inches deep after an average of 3.87 putts.

ball-drop area

An extremely large divot
outlined in white into
which a ball may be
dropped to replace one
lost in an adjacent hazard.
See HAZARD.

ballwasher

Handy noisemaking device located on the tees of most golf holes as a convenience for players who have no car keys or loose change in their pockets to rattle during an opponent's backswing.

ballwasher

banana ball

1. Wild slice hit by a would-be gorilla swinging like a monkey. *2.* Formal dance at a WASP country club.

best ball Tournament format in which only the lowest score of a foursome needs to be fudged, and rather than cheating individually, all the players team up to cheat as a group.

better ball

Tournament format in which the lower of two scores made by a twosome on a hole is entered in the column of the scorecard under the name of the player with the highest handicap.

birdie A mulligan, the best of one or more "practice swings," and a 20-foot "gimme" putt. *See* EAGLE.

bite

1. Descriptive term for the way a ball "sucks back" after hitting a green due to powerful backspin applied by an expert golfer. *2.* Identical term with a different meaning used to describe bad shots hit by hackers which also "bite" and "suck."

A DUFFER'S DICTIONARY | 23

blind hole A hole
whose green is not visible from
the tee, thus requiring a player
to rely on senses other than
sight, such as the sound of
an unseen golfer cursing after
being struck by a ball, the smell
of trouble, the taste of fear, and
the feel of the soft moss during
a crawl through the woods.

body English

Informal term for vigorous leaning or twisting movements that players make to "persuade" a ball to go in the desired direction. If these antics fail to have the intended effect, they are often followed by a series of vulgar hand and arm motions known as body Spanish, body French, or body Italian.

bogey The number of strokes taken on a hole recorded by a golfer of average skill and above-average honesty. *See* DOUBLE BOGEY and PENALTY STROKE.

borrow The amount of break in a putt, which can be decreased by repeatedly lifting the ball from the green, marking it, and replacing it closer to the hole in a process known as the "steal."

bounce A sudden kick or rebound made by a ball that is either totally and completely unfair or just exactly what you intended.

brassie

brassie
Old name for the 2-wood, which often had a brass sole-plate. The 3-wood was once known as a "spoon," the 4-wood as a "baffie," and the 7-iron as a "mashie-niblick." A club wrapped around a tree is a "smashie." If it is flung into a water hazard, it is a "splashie." If it has a slippery grip, it is a "bashie." And any club allegedly used to score a hole-in-one is a "fibstick" if it's an iron or a "fablespoon" if it's a wood.

bunker

A hazard consisting of an area of ground along a fairway or adjacent to a green from which soil has been removed and replaced with something designed to trap golfers. If such a hazard occupies more than 2,000 square feet and traps golfers permanently, it is referred to as a "condominium."

buried lie Descriptive term for a ball sitting down so deeply in the rough that it is almost impossible to get a shoe on it. See IMPOSSIBLE LIE.

caddy Individual employed by players who are unable to select the wrong club, misread putts, or lose balls without assistance. See FORECADDY.

caddy

Calamity Jane

Legendary golfer Bobby Jones' nickname for his "straight-shooting" putter. Contemporary players rarely name their putters, but those who do are likely to choose less appreciative monikers like "Runaround Sue," "Unsinkable Molly Brown," "Little Miss Muffet," or "Lizzie Borden."

carry The distance a ball needs to travel to cross a hazard, either in the air or in a pocket or the palm of a hand.

casual water

Temporary accumulation of water. The rules of golf permit a ball to be moved without penalty from any nonpermanent wet area, such as a rain puddle. Tears, however, no matter how copious, do not constitute casual water.

chip-and-run

A low approach shot in which a ball is hit in the air about one-third of the way to the pin and then permitted to roll the remaining twelve-thirds of the distance to the hole.

chip shot A delicate run-up shot with a flat trajectory that gets a player into position for one or more missed putts. *See* PITCH.

chip shot

choke *1.* To grip down on the shaft of a club. *2.* To blow a lead after being needled by an opponent. *3.* To grip down on his neck.

clubhead covers

Wool or leather "mittens" slipped over the heads and shafts of graphite woods to protect them from damage. Zip-on coverings that encase the entire club in wetsuit material are also available which permit the eventual reuse of a favorite club flung into a water hazard, assuming that blind rage was tempered by foresight.

comebacker Slang

term for a putt that ends
up a foot short of the hole
after the "flybyer" ran four
feet past it, but before
the "edgeburner" lips out
on the low side of the cup.
See KNEEKNOCKER.

concede To generously permit an opponent to pick up a putt that just hopped out of the hole, or came to rest against the pin, or cannot be marked without the coin falling into the cup. See GIMME.

course management

Term for a basic businesslike playing strategy in which blame for bad shots is assigned to club employees and fellow players, disappointing results are adjusted to appear more favorable, and every effort possible is made to drive competitors into bankruptcy.

crosshanded
Term for a reversed putting grip with the strong hand above the weaker hand whose chief advantage is that trying to make any kind of stroke with this awkward and unnatural method of holding the club gives a player a more pressing problem to occupy his mind than worrying about holing the ball, as well as something obvious to blame when he doesn't.

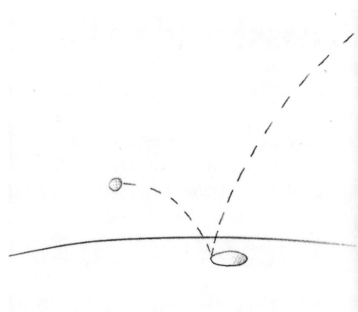

cup

cup The metal or plastic cylinder fitted into the hole in the green. Strictly speaking, it is only the *liner* of the hole, but in everyday golf usage players will often say "cup" when they mean "hole," much as they frequently say "just in bounds" when they mean "out of bounds," "Oh, here it is" when they mean "I can't find it," and "five" when they mean "seven."

cure The solution to yesterday's problem and the source of tomorrow's collapse. See INSTRUCTION and LESSON TEE.

dance floor
Slang term for the surface of the putting green, where players perform the Breakdown, the Can't-Can't, the Double Boogaloo, the Fling, the Funky Chicken, the Hokey-Pokey, the Heel-and-Toe, the Hustle, the Mexican Hat Dance, the Monkey, the Reel, the Shake, the Shimmy, the Shuffle, the Snake Dance, the Three-Step, the Turkey Trot, and the Twist.

dead Familiar term for a putt so short it is almost impossible to believe you missed it.

dimples Telltale patterns of tiny circular hollows on the covers of golf balls that gives them aerodynamic lift and helps players identify a ball in deep rough as theirs even if it has changed its brand, number, and logo.

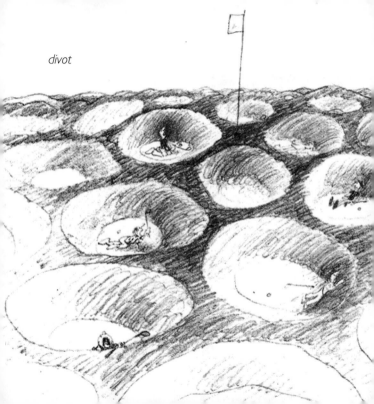

divot

divot

The piece of turf scooped from the ground by a stroke made with an iron. Many players are frustrated golf architects, and they welcome the chance to try their hand at course design by leaving the divot holes unrepaired, thus creating unexpected and devilish little sand traplets and minibunkers right in the middle of the fairway to provide interesting challenges for their fellow golfers.

dogleg A hole with a sharply angled fairway which, depending on whether it turns to the right or turns to the left, will immediately cure a slice or instantly eliminate a hook.

do-over A first shot that a player inadvertently hit second. See MULLIGAN and RE-TEE.

double bogey

Two strokes over par, or, for a golfer who ended up with a 7 on a long par 5, a back-to-back birdie and eagle that he happened to score on the same hole. See TRIPLE BOGEY.

double eagle

Three strokes less than par for a given hole. This unusual achievement might be accomplished, say, by taking advantage of a tailwind on a straight downhill par 5 to get down in two strokes, or scoring a hole-in-one on a short par 4, or carding a zero by just skipping entirely a difficult par 3.

downswing The

portion of the golf swing during which the club is swept down toward the ball, which most players execute just after addressing the ball but well before the beginning of the backswing.

draw Term commonly
used by golfers to describe
a snap-hooked ball they
were actually able to find.
See FADE.

dress   PRO   AMATEUR

dress Although clothes in a variety of styles are acceptable on a golf course, a few general pointers are worth keeping in mind when selecting an outfit:

- It should be visible to an individual with normal eyesight looking out the window of a spacecraft in orbit.

- It should be made out of a fabric woven from a substance that was mined or refined rather than grown or raised.
- It should require dry cleaning and dissolve or disintegrate if washed.
- It should be composed of no fewer than eight separate colors or shades and should have at least four distinct emblems.

- It should make the wearer look shorter and fatter.
- It should jam radar.
- When scuffed, the shoes worn with the outfit should require repainting or restuccoing rather than a shining.
- Any hat should be identifiable as such only by its position on the wearer's head.

drive The shot that comes after the whiff and before the mulligan. See HONOR and ONE-WOOD.

driver Wood club with the longest shaft and least loft that is carried by most golfers solely for the purpose of making the slightly shorter and marginally deeper-faced 3-wood seem easy to hit.

driving range

A place where golfers
go to get all the good
shots out of their systems.
See PRACTICE TEE.

driving range

drop The act of replacing a lost or unplayable ball in which a golfer holds a ball at arm's length and lets it slip from his hand while simultaneously letting the penalty stroke slip from his mind.

dropkick A drive in which the clubhead hits the ground before the ball, producing a shot that barely makes it to the 50-yard line before it is whistled dead.

duffer A golfer who is much more likely to shoot his own weight than his age.

dying putt A putt that did not sink but came to rest right at the hole, as opposed to a putt that ran way by and still has a long and challenging life ahead of it full of many hard knocks and ups and downs.

eagle Unusually low score on a hole achieved by a golfer with an exceptionally good drive and one or two exceptionally good follow-up shots, or by a golfer with an exceptionally poor memory. *See* HOLE-IN-ONE and SCORECARD.

equipment According
to the rules of golf, equipment is "anything that can be thrown, broken, kicked, twisted, torn, crushed, shredded, or mangled; or propelled, driven, or directed, either under its own power or by means of a transfer of momentum, into underbrush, trees, or other overgrown terrain, or over the edge of a natural or artificially elevated area, or below the surface of any body of water, whether moving or impounded."

etiquette (Don't spoil the surprises.)

etiquette The rules of
behavior in golf. The most important
ones are:
- Don't talk on your own backswing.
- Don't sneeze into a borrowed glove.
- Don't needle your partner.
- Don't cut in on the middle of a par 3.
- Don't write in ink on the scorecard.
- Don't give range balls as Christmas
  presents.
- If your opponent is new to the course,
  don't spoil the surprises.

explosion shot

A bunker shot that causes players to blow up and their scores to explode. See SAND TRAP and SAND WEDGE.

fade Term commonly used by golfers to describe a wildly sliced ball that somehow managed to stay in bounds. See HOOK & SLICE.

fairway

fairway A narrow strip of closely mown grass that separates two groups of golfers looking for lost balls in the rough.

fairway wood

A club with a medium loft that is used to get a ball out of a good lie on the fairway and into position for a shot from a slope, a bunker, a water hazard, or the back of a tree.

fat Term for a shot that results when the clubhead hits a ball 7,900 miles in diameter prior to contacting the 1.62-inch-diameter golf ball. See SCLAFF.

finesse shot Any nonstandard shot used to get a ball out of an awkward or impossible lie by bending, twisting, or stretching the rules or by hitting it directly through a loophole.

flagstick

Long, flexible metal pole with striped markings along its length and a numbered flag at its top which would have marked the position of the hole if the previous playing group hadn't left it lying on the green.

flight

The intended path a ball would have followed through the air if delays, bad weather, or unexpected mechanical problems hadn't caused it to be diverted to another destination.

fluff A shot that is too weak to be registered by conventional scorekeeping equipment. See WHIFF.

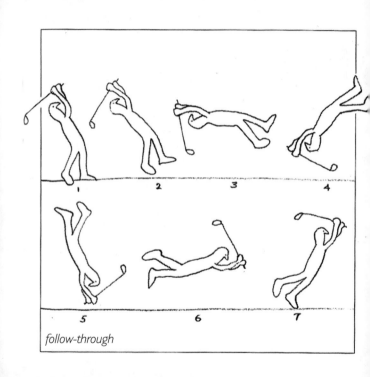

follow-through

follow-through

The part of the swing that takes place after the ball has been hit but before the club has been thrown.

Fore! The first of several four-letter words exchanged between golfers as one group of players hits balls into another group.

Fore!

forecaddy A caddy sent ahead on a hole so he can immediately signal that he doesn't have a clue where an errant drive ended up instead of wasting five minutes pretending to know where it landed.

forward press

A lateral shift of the hips or hands or knees toward the target that many golfers use to initiate the swing after using the head of the club to apply a lie-enhancing move known as the "downward press" to the turf directly behind the ball.

four-ball A match in which four golfers each play their own balls until they have lost every one of them, at which point play shifts to a "no ball" format and they head to the clubhouse for a round of gin rummy.

foursome
Four golfers playing a round together. Three golfers are a threesome, and two form a twosome. Four ladies playing slowly are a "gruesome." Four men playing after a long lunch at the 19th hole are a "fearsome." A single attractive woman playing alone is a "toothsome." A husband

and wife playing together are a "quarrelsome." A group of golfers who give advice while watching another group tee off is a "meddlesome." A single player with a large number of old jokes is a "tiresome." And two younger men playing a fast, sub-par round are a "loathsome."

foursome

front nine
The first half of an 18-hole golf course. A golfer who, by the end of the 9th hole, has shot within a few strokes of par for 18 is entitled to skip the second half of the course and head directly for the 19th hole.

game A competitive round of golf, often with a friendly wager, with nothing much riding on the outcome other than life or death.

gimme

gimme
A putt so short there's no way you would have missed the damn thing if the stingy S.O.B. you're playing with had been enough of a sportsman to concede it. *See* GIVE-GIVE.

give-give Slang term for an equitable mutual arrangement between two players in which each concedes to the other a putt that both of them had an equally minuscule chance of making. *See* GOOD.

golf

The derivation of the word "golf" from its Celtic and Middle English roots is obscure. Some possibilities are: *gilff* (an incurable madness), *gylf* (a notorious liar), *gullf* (to beat a shrub with a stick), *golve* (under; beneath; lost; blocked; submerged; obstructed), *galfa* (my God!; oh, no!), *goulfyl* (to cry; to weep), and *gaelfu* (I quit).

golf accessory

A gadget whose purchase improves players' games primarily by eliminating bulk from their wallets, thereby reducing excessive trouser friction and allowing a smoother hip movement in the swing.

golf bag Portable fabric or leather sacklike container designed to hold clubs between throws. See TRAVEL COVER.

golf cart
Four-wheeled electric or gas-powered vehicle that decreases the exercise value of playing 18 holes of golf from about the level of two sets of doubles tennis or a 5-mile hike to the equivalent of an hour of vigorous shopping.

golf cart

golf club

1. Basic implement in golf, consisting of a long shaft with a head on one end, which is attached to the shaft at the heel and has on one side a distinct face. *2.* Social organization composed of a number of heels, a membership committee head with two faces, and a long waiting list of people who are going to get the shaft.

golf course A place where people who are cooped up in the office all week go to get a chance to lie and cheat outdoors.

golf trip A playing holiday spent in a place where no one can ever remember when it got so hot so early, or snowed so late, or rained so much.

golf trip

golf widow

Nonplaying wife of golfer. Just for the record, judges have consistently ruled that although golf is a form of "extreme mental cruelty," it is not grounds for divorce since "the sufferings are experienced exclusively by the player and not by the one abandoned as the result of such play."

good Familiar term for a putt short enough to concede. Such putts are usually measured in inches, like a 6-inch putt, or a 12-inch putt, or a 24-inch putt, or a 48-inch putt, or a 96-inch putt, or a 144-inch putt. *See* IN THE LEATHER.

go to school

To study the speed or break of a green by observing another player's putt along a line similar to the one your ball is going to travel, usually followed by a trip to the principal's office for a brief lecture on the importance of staying awake during class.

grain
The direction the grass on a putting green grows, which produces a deviation in the roll of the ball that would have caused your putt to miss the cup by several inches if the slope hadn't already sent it 10 feet past the hole.

green Roughly circular expanse of tightly mown and smoothly rolled grass approximately three putts long and four putts wide. See READING THE GREEN.

green

greens fees
The charge for playing a round of golf. When paying this sum, mediocre players should keep in mind the fact that whereas golfers who routinely shoot par are shelling out as much as $2 for every shot they take, a hopeless duffer often pays less than 50¢ a stroke.

grip *1.* Rubber or leather sheath on the end of a club that players change once or twice a year. *2.* Method of positioning the hands on the club that players change once or twice a week.

Ground Under Repair

Marked portion of the course undergoing restoration or alteration from which players may move their ball from a bad lie without penalty, an action that is normally possible only in Ground Not Currently Under Observation.

half-shot A shot made with a partial swing that ends up exactly the same distance short of a hole as a full shot with less club.

ham & egg

Slang term for the perfectly complementary play of two partners in a better-ball match, one of whom always manages to get a good score on a hole whenever the other one ends up with a bad one. When both players keep getting good scores or bad scores on the same hole, their play is known as "hummus-and-eggplant," "bologna-and-meatball," "tuna-and-noodle," or "turkey-and-dumpling." *See* PARTNER.

handicap An allocation of strokes on one or more holes that permits two golfers of very different ability to do equally poorly on the same golf course. *See* SANDBAGGER.

hazard

hazard

An obstacle on the course, either a bunker or a water hazard. It is against the rules for players to "ground" their clubs in a hazard by allowing the head of the club to touch the sand or water before making their shots. However, prior to taking a stroke, a player is permitted to hang his head, bury his head in his hands, and, if it does not unduly delay the match, lightly and repeatedly pound his head against a tree.

head

1. The part of the club designed to hit the ball. *2.* The part of the player designed to make it next to impossible to hit the ball. *See* MIND GAME.

hickory

Tough, resilient wood originally used for golf club shafts. Modern graphite and steel shafts are stronger and more durable, but old-time golfers insist that there is nothing more satisfying than the crisp snap of a hickory-shafted club being broken sharply across the knee or the delicate aroma of an entire set of clubs burning merrily in a fireplace.

hole

hole

The small, circular hollow cut into the green that is the objective of play and the only deep, steep-sided piece of ground on the course into which a ball will not immediately roll if it lands anywhere near it.

hole-in-one
A ball hit directly from the tee into the hole on a single shot by a golfer playing alone.

hole out Archaic term
for the quaint, antiquated
custom of completing a
hole by actually sinking,
rather than picking up, the
final short- to medium-
length putt.

home course

A place where your chief handicap is that everyone knows exactly what it is. See SANDBAGGER.

honor The privilege of being laughed at first on the tee. See SKIED DRIVE.

hook & slice

To hit a shot that for a right-hander curves sharply left (hook) or right (slice), respectively. Players who do one or the other consistently should consider changing the way they stand, grip the club, or make their swing. Players who do both should consider changing the way they spend their weekends.

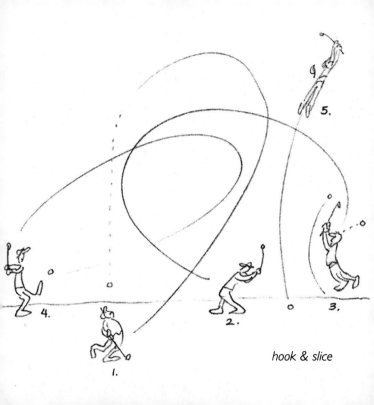

hook & slice

hosel The socket on the clubhead where the shaft goes into the neck of an iron and the shank goes into the middle of the woods.

impossible lie

The position of a ball that is both completely obstructed by an immovable object and continuously observed by an incorruptible player.

instruction

Any coaching, teaching, or tutoring as a result of which a golfer manages to eliminate the one glaring fault that perfectly compensated for all his other swing flaws.

instruction

in the leather

Phrase indicating that a putt is to be
conceded because the ball is closer
to the hole than to the end of the
leather grip of a putter laid along the
line of the putt, or a player standing
near the hole is close enough to the
ball to kick it away with a leather golf
shoe or pick it up in a leather golf glove.

in the pocket

Phrase used to describe a situation when a player has picked up his ball once a high score has taken him out of a hole, or when, due to the presence in his pocket of a ball identical to the one he has been fruitlessly searching for, a player is about to miraculously get back into a hole.

iron One of about a dozen blade-shaped metal-headed clubs with progressively greater lofts that are designed to hit the ball 10 yards short of the green or 20 yards past it.

junior A golfer who attributes his or her poor play to the fact that he or she lacks the experience of a mature player. *See* SENIOR.

kick A bounce of the ball in an unfavorable direction, usually followed by a somewhat delayed but much more favorable second kick.

kneeknocker

Slang term for a short but highly missable putt also known as a headshaker, a tearjerker, a browslapper, a hatflinger, a clubslammer, or a caddyblamer.

knockdown A low punched shot that is extremely useful when the wind is very strong or play is very slow.

ladies' tees The place from which women hit their drives and men hit their second shots.

lag The first quarter of a four-putt.

lateral shot

Polite term for a shank,
the only golf shot you
can immediately master
simply by watching
someone hit one.

lay-up
A shot that would have stopped safely short of a hazard, a line of trees, a ravine, or some other trouble on a hole if you hadn't used a nice easy swing that knocked the ball 30 yards farther than you ever hit that club in your entire life.

legs

A ball is said to have "legs" if it continues to roll a long way after landing. If it bounces quickly into the rough, it has "hooves." If it becomes wedged under a rock or in the roots of a tree, it has "claws." If it runs down a bank and into a water hazard, it has "fins." And if it does all these things on the same hole, it is given "wings" and flung into the underbrush.

lesson tee

The place where players
go to convert a wicked
slice into a nasty hook.

lie *1.* Where the ball comes to rest after being hit by a golfer. *2.* The number of strokes it took to get it there, as reported by that golfer.

links

links Traditional seaside golf course consisting of 18 holes that play into the wind and located in the middle of a 200-acre unplayable lie.

lip *1.* Perimeter of grass surrounding the hole. *2.* Remarks made by fellow golfer when your putt stops there. See RIM.

local rules

A set of regulations that are ignored only by players on one specific course rather than by golfers as a whole. See RULES OF GOLF.

loft
The angle of a clubface and the corresponding steepness of the shot it will produce. Loft angles range from the relatively shallow ones used for long, unobstructed shots (12° for a driver, 20° for a fairway wood, 30° for a 5-iron) to the much steeper ones needed to clear obstacles (47° for a 9-iron, 58° for a sand wedge, 75° for the tip of a golf shoe, and up to 100° for a throwing arm).

loose impediments

Natural and legally movable objects that interfere with play, such as dazed or disoriented reptiles or mammals, stunned birds, pulverized stones, flattened bushes, uprooted shrubs, severed branches, and felled trees. *See* OBSTRUCTIONS.

lost ball

lost ball An opponent's missing ball after 10 seconds of searching, or one of yours after 15 minutes.

mallet Heavy-headed putter that many players prefer because it seems to help control the yips, and if it fails to do so, it can be thrown twice as far as a conventional blade putter. *See* YIPS.

marker Any small, flat, round object, such as a coin, used to indicate a spot on a putting green approximately 6 inches closer to the hole than the position from which the ball was lifted.

match A hole-by-hole golfing competition in which your skill is pitted against your opponent's luck. See NASSAU.

medal play

A golfing competition whose outcome is determined by the total number of strokes forgotten during an entire round.

member-guest

Club tournament usually won as a result of supernatural play by an old army buddy or one of the members who just got a little lucky and managed to shoot a Gross Score equal to his USGA Handicap Index of 38 on the back nine.

mind game

The 90% of golf that is
mental as opposed to the
10% that is psychological.

mixed foursome

A quartet of golfers
composed of two separate
grounds for divorce.

mulligan
An additional ball or balls a player is permitted to hit, without penalty, on the opening hole of a round, based on the sound principle that the first tee is an extension of the driving range, and the line to be crossed between "practice" and "play" lies approximately 200 yards out in the middle of the first fairway.

Nassau Popular golf bet in
which points are awarded on
the front and back nines and
after the 18-hole round to the
player who made the fewest
strokes on the course or
obtained the most strokes
on the first tee.

needle Do you always move your lips when you read? Don't you ever buy any serious books? Is golf all you ever think about?

19th hole

19th hole

The only hole on which players do not complain about the number of shots they took.

numbers
A player's score after the subtraction of his or her handicap from the Gross Score is the Net Score. Adding strokes for each mulligan yields the True Score. If whiffs and fluffs are also counted, the resulting tabulation is the Real Score. If strokes for lost balls, improved lies, and shots hit out of bounds are included as well, the grand total is the Actual Score. This number, when adjusted upward to reflect all gimme putts, becomes the

Correct Score. When all the strokes
made in sand traps and around
obstructions are tacked on, this larger
sum is the Absolute, Final, Honest-to-
Goodness Score, which is usually only
a half-dozen or so strokes lower than
the total number of shots the player in
fact made. See SCOREBOARD.

obstructions

obstructions

Golfers may move their ball away from or remove any artificial obstacles not part of the course such as torn and crushed hats and other discarded articles of clothing; chewed scorecards; ripped instruction books; halved golf balls; discarded golf clubs; demolished handcarts; and overturned and burning electric carts.

official records

The history of golf is filled with the memorable accomplishments of the game's stars, but, alas, the more humble achievements of less skilled players often go unsung. The brief list below is an attempt to rectify this unfortunate state of affairs.

SHORTEST MISSED PUTT: .83 inch, Randall P. Huggins, 9th green, Gossiping Pines C.C., Bedham, Mass., 1977

LONGEST SUSTAINED SCREAM: 39 seconds, Liz Yownes, 8th tee, Tallulah Lake C.C., Los Nachos, Calif., 1982

SHARPEST SHAFT BEND IN ONE MOTION: 314°, A. McNaith, 14th hole, Napping River C.C., Necco, Ont., 1968

FARTHEST THROWN CLUB: 86.4 yards, B. Bob Binger, windmill hole, Tumbleweed Putt 'n' Sup, Zeno, Tex., 1974

one-putt To send the ball into the hole with one stroke of a putter after taking 11 shots to reach the green. *See* FOUR-PUTT.

one-wood The only commonly used alternative name for the driver that is suitable for printing.

out of bounds

out of bounds

Beyond the boundary markers. A shot hit O.B. ("oh-bee") may not be played, but exceptions are often made for a ball that ends up J.A.L.O.B. ("jah-loh-bee"—Just A Little Out of Bounds), or I.T.O.-W.Y.C.K.I.B.I.B. ("itoh-wicki-bib"—In the Open Where You Can Kick It Back In Bounds), or W.O.B.I.S.B.Y.B.I.L.L.N.O.H. ("woh-bee-isby-bill-noh"—Way Out of Bounds In Someone's Back Yard, But It Looks Like No One's Home).

overclubbing & underclubbing

Terms for common errors in club selection that can be easily corrected by overlooking or undercounting the resulting errant shots.

par Score achieved by a golfer who had only a few great shots on an entire round but somehow managed to hit them all on the same hole. *See* TRIPLE BOGEY.

partner Match-play team member who holes out from a bunker to score a birdie on a hole you were about to win with a tap-in for a par, then putts out for a double bogey on a hole where you lie six, and your ball is 40 feet from the cup.

partner

penalty stroke

One or more strokes added to a golfer's score as punishment for conspicuous, excessive, brazen, or shameless displays of honesty, fair play, and sportsmanship completely at odds with the spirit of the game of golf.

pin

Familiar term for the flagstick. A ball that lands on the green parallel to the hole but off to one side is "pin high." A ball that lands right next to the hole, leaving a very short putt, is said to be "stiff to the pin." Such putts are almost always conceded, but some players insist on putting them anyway. These players are known as "pinheads."

pin position

1. The place 40 feet away from your ball on the other side of the green where the flagstick sits in the cup, indicating the current hole location. 2. The place right next to your ball where a circular turf plug or dab of white paint marks the spot where the hole was yesterday or will be tomorrow.

pitch A lofted shot that flies over a hazard between the ball and the hole and into a bunker on the other side of the green.

pitch-and-putt

A short par-3 course, also known as a pitch-and-moan, a yank-and-yip, a shank-and-stab, or a sclaff-and-lip.

Play it as it lays

One of the three
fundamental dictates
of golf. The others are
"Wear it if it clashes" and
"Steal it if it has stopped
rolling."

playing through

playing through

A display of courtesy on the course in which a group of golfers who have stopped to search for lost balls conclude that they are causing delay and, anxious to spare the players behind them a wait of several minutes on the tee, stand aside and invite that group to hit their drives so they will be able to profitably use the period of time before they can resume play in a lengthy search for their own lost balls.

plumb bob To survey the slope of a green by sighting along the shaft of a putter suspended perpendicular to the ground, a technique that ensures that even on lightning-fast putting surfaces every putt is going to take a very, very long time.

practice green

Warm-up putting surface that is twice as slow or three times faster than any actual green on the course.

practice tee

Mysterious place found on most golf courses where for some unknown reason players who are incapable of hitting 97 shots in under 5 hours can easily hit 100 balls in less than 10 minutes.

press

Descriptive term for a strategy involving an additional double-or-nothing bet over the remaining holes of a match negotiated by a player who is already too far behind to have any chance of winning the original stakes, but is not yet close enough to the parking lot to change the game into a nothing-or-nothing wager with a maneuver known as a "stiff," a "slip," or a "welsh."

priority
In determining the order of play, the following rules should apply:

- Matches which, when mulligans, do-overs, and practice shots are included, are playing 10, 12, or 14 balls should give way to matches playing 6 or 8 balls.

- A match playing the course out of sequence by cutting over from the green of one hole to the tee of a later hole is entitled to pass a match that sneaked onto the course without paying.

- Any match that has a player in it posing as a doctor late for a vital operation takes precedence over a match with a player pretending to be a judge late for a key trial.
- Single players have no standing on the course and must give way to a two-some, threesome, or foursome unless, through voice changes and swing variations, they can convincingly fake the symptoms of a multiple personality disorder.

pro-am Charity golf tournament in which mid- to high handicappers who spend most of their golfing lives playing with a bunch of inconsiderate jerks who can't break 100 get a chance to play a round of golf with an inconsiderate jerk who can easily break 70.

professional

A player who believes that
if you're going to have a
miserable time on a golf
course you might as well
get paid for it.

pro shop

pro shop The only place on a golf course where players fervently hope they won't end up breaking a hundred.

provisional ball

A second "back-up" drive knocked deep into the woods just in case the first ball yanked into the high rough can't be found.

pull & push

Absolutely straight, perfectly hit, unbelievably solid shots that fly incredibly far in entirely the wrong direction.

putt

One or more gentle tapping strokes made with a short club with a flat face used to roll the ball toward the cup, and a cavity back employed to scoop it up off the green when it gets close enough to the hole that a fellow player would be more embarrassed to make you putt it than you are to pick it up.

putt

putter Specialized club used on the green that differs from the other golf clubs in a player's bag in that it *always* produces shots that just trickle along the ground a few feet before stopping.

quoits Along with curling, racing in luges and tossing the caber, the only game other than golf that has been voted Most Pointless Athletic Pursuit of the Decade more than three times by the editors of *Stupid Sports* magazine.

raingear Lightweight, waterproof clothing that would have provided a player excellent protection from a sudden downpour out on the course if it weren't in the trunk of his car.

rake Implement used for smoothing sand in bunkers whose handle deflected your ball into a set of deep footprints a few inches from where its head is resting.

reading the

green
Putting surfaces are seldom level, and golfers must study them closely to learn which way they break. Even the "friendliest"-looking green will have some tricks up its sleeve, and many are downright ornery. Thus, the message of any given green can range from "Aim three balls outside the left edge" to "You'll be lucky to get down in four, and those are the ugliest pants I have ever seen."

reading the green

recovery shot

A challenging shot successfully played from a difficult lie or unfavorable position to a place from which it is possible to three-putt.

regulation Term used

by a golfer to describe his
pure-par play during a
round when he always
reached the greens in one,
two, three, er, um, or ah
strokes, and holed out with
twoish putts.

relief Unusual situation when, thanks to the rules of golf, a player is actually able to improve his lie without counting a penalty stroke while another golfer is watching.

rescue club

A specially designed utility club, often a lofted fairway wood or hybrid iron-wood, that allows players who would normally have to chip out into the fairway from a terrible lie on one side of the hole to hit the ball into another terrible lie 200 yards away.

re-tee
To make a second drive. Because the tee shot requires intense concentration, a player is almost always permitted to hit another ball, without penalty, providing the original mishit was caused by some obvious interference like the clicking of another golfer's shoelaces together, or the sudden wingflash of a passing butterfly, or the nearby impact of a subatomic particle.

rim The edge of the hole. A ball that goes around the cup without falling in is said to have rimmed the hole, or to have ringed, skirted, lipped, lapped, or looped it. It may also be said to have curled, circled, or rolled around it, or to have done a tour, a circuit, a round trip, an orbit, or a buttonhook. There are one or two terms for a ball actually going into the cup, but they are used so seldom that it seems like a waste of space to include them here.

rough

Unmown, naturally wild area bordering the fairway and sometimes separating the fairway from the tee. There are three basic types of rough: low rough, a narrow strip of 6-inch-high grass where the ball may be easily playable; high or deep rough, where the ball may be lost and, even if found, may be obstructed or otherwise unplayable; and U.S. Open rough, where the ball may be eaten or stolen and used as an object of worship by primitive peoples.

rough

round Eighteen holes of golf, played in their proper sequence, followed by one or more rounds at the 19th hole.

rules of golf

The 34 basic rules of golf, as opposed to the 92 exemptions, 148 major modifications, and 1,146 special exceptions.

sandbagger Golf

hustler with a fraudulent handicap
who wins matches by pretending to be a poorer player than
he really is. It can be hard to spot
these con men, but here are a
few warning signs:

- A tee tucked behind the ear
- A nervous habit of bouncing
  the ball on the face of a 5-iron

- A set of banged-up clubs without headcovers, with a 1-iron, four wedges, and a putter that looks like a fireplace tool
- A hat with the logo of a manufacturer of motor oil
- A bag tag from a golf club in Waco, Texas
- A towel stolen from a motel
- Running shoes

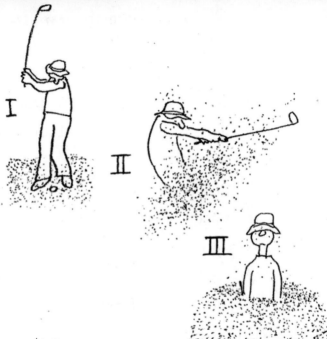

I

II

III

sand trap

sand trap A deep depression filled with sand filled with golfers in a deep depression.

sand wedge

Remarkably versatile iron with a high loft, a heavy clubhead, and a deeply flanged sole used to hit tricky shots from sand or deep grass around the green anywhere from 5 to 275 yards.

sclaff

Onomatopoetic Scottish word for a flubbed shot in which the ground is contacted before the ball is hit. The game of golf's Gaelic originators had dozens of words for specific golf shots, like a shot chunked into water (*sloch*), a shot popped up into a bunker (*footh*), a shot snap-hooked into trees (*brattle*), a shot skulled into tall grass (*whirrip*), a shot sliced into another playing group (*smachdoon*), and a shot hit perfectly (*a fecking miracle*).

scorecard

A preprinted listing of the holes on the course on which a player records his opening offer prior to the commencement of serious negotiations.

scorecard

scramble Tournament format in which all the members of a foursome drive and then hit successive shots from the ball position of the player with the best lie or the loudest mouth.

scrambling golf

Style of play in which a golfer ends up with a respectable score in spite of, rather than because of, the shots he hit.

scratch player

scratch player

A player with a handicap
of zero; a par golfer; a rat;
a louse; a stinker.

senior A golfer who attributes his poor play to the fact that he lacks the physique of a younger player. *See* JUNIOR.

sh–nk One of two five-letter words that it is a far more serious breach of etiquette to utter on a golf course than any four-letter word. The other is ch–ke.

short game

The short shots played around the green (chips, putts, pitches, and sand trap blasts) and the cheap shots taken between the green and the next tee (quips, digs, cracks, slams, and jests).

shotmaking

The ability to make dumb luck look like smart play. See RECOVERY SHOT and RESCUE CLUB.

skied drive

Tee shot with a very high trajectory that often fails to clear a hazard or a waste area. Also known as a ballooned drive, a rainmaker, a moon shot, a test shot, a trial balloon, a canceled shot, a jettisoned stroke, or a rescheduled launch.

skied drive

spin
Professional golfers and other accomplished players can apply a variety of spins to the ball to make it curve around obstacles, bore into the wind, stop dead where it lands, or even reverse direction. These shots take skill and practice, but most beginners have a bag of tricks, too. For example, even

the rankest of amateurs can
amaze their playing companions
by making a ball run right across
the center of a hole without
going in, rise straight up into
the air, execute unbelievably
sharp left or right turns, travel
sideways or even backwards,
or disappear entirely.

Stableford

Scoring system in which players are awarded a progressively greater number of points for pars, birdies, and eagles. A similar system called "GeraldFord," widely used in charity tournaments, awards players points for the number of spectators they hit.

stance

The placement of a player's feet in relation to the ball and the target line in the brief period just prior to the beginning of the swing while they are still positioned inside his shoes.

Stimpmeter
Device used to measure the speed of the greens on a golf course. Similar instruments include the hackometer, which computes the length of the rough; the inertial slomoscope, which assesses the speed of play; the gas chromograph, which rates the digestibility of the

food in the halfway house; the gougegauge, which calculates the markup of the prices in the pro shop; and the asshologram, which appraises the unpleasantness of the club members.

streak A score of par on two consecutive holes, or one birdie in a row.

stroke Any forward
motion of the club that
is made with the intention
of hitting the ball and is
observed by another golfer.

sudden death

Term for the situation that exists when a match is tied at the end of 18 holes and the player who feels the least amount of confidence in the outcome of a playoff suddenly remembers the death, earlier in the day, of a beloved aunt.

sweet spot

The specific place on a clubface that produces maximum accuracy and power and a solid feeling of perfect contact when a ball is struck. This point varies from club to club, but generally speaking it's in the dead center of the "bland belt," which is very near the "rotten region," in the middle of the "lousy area," and surrounded by the "loathsome zone."

swing key A simple thought, concept, or idea that improves a player's swing for more than 15 minutes or a minimum of three holes.

swingweight

A measurement of the relationship between the weight of the clubhead and the weight of the shaft used to indicate the "feel" of the club. A separate pair of measurements evaluates the shaft's ability to communicate a finger-stinging shock when an iron is sharply topped on a cold day (stingweight) and the ease with which the club can be thrown (flingweight).

takeaway The initial stage of the backswing when any chance of hitting a decent shot is removed entirely.

takeaway

tap-in A putt short enough to lip out with a one-handed stroke or rocket past the hole with a left-handed slap with the back of the putter.

target line

An imaginary line from
a player's lie to the target
which the ball would follow
if an imaginary golfer hit it.

tee Small wooden peg on which
the ball is placed for a drive
from the teeing ground. The
condition of the tee after the
shot provides an indication
of whether or not the ball
was hit correctly. If the tee flips
backwards and lands in one
piece a few inches behind the
place where it was inserted into

the turf, the ball was probably hit well. If the tee breaks into three or more pieces, is driven deeper than two inches into the ground, travels farther than the ball, or catches fire, it probably wasn't.

teeing ground

A clearly defined rectangular area 2 club-lengths in depth from which players hit shots 20 to 30 dub-lengths directly forward or 5 to 10 flub-lengths to either side.

tee off To drive a ball off a tee. Players who have made their drives off a tee are said to *have* teed off, but at this point it is almost always also correct to say that they *are* teed off.

tempo The rhythm or timing of a swing. Most skilled golfers pace their swings with a deliberate count of "one-*and*-two"; most hackers pace their swings with an immediate count of "*TWO!*"

tempo

Texas wedge

Slang term for a putter used to hit a low, running shot from well off the green. Similar terms are "Florida Putter" for a driver used to hit a weak, half-topped shot that doesn't reach the Ladies' Tee, and "Myrtle Beach Driving Iron" for a skulled sand wedge that sends a ball out of a bunker and into the middle of an adjacent fairway.

tight lie Term for a

situation in which the ball comes
to rest on very short grass or a
bald spot or hardpan, a position
also known as a "close lie," an
"original lie," a "preliminary lie,"
a "previous lie," or a "former lie."

tip A free piece of advice offered by a fellow player, which is the only thing in the entire game of golf that is worth exactly as much as you paid for it.

titanium Lightweight, superstrong metal used in clubheads whose superior impact power has made it possible for older or less skilled players to hit shots into hazards, fairway bunkers, water areas, and maintenance sheds they never dreamed of reaching before.

top To hit the ball well above its centerline, causing it to hop or skitter a few yards forward, a problem that usually afflicts only beginning golfers and is quickly left behind once a player has learned to master the stub, the fat shot, and the chili dip.

travel cover Durable, impact-resistant case designed to protect a set of golf clubs from damage while being transported by an airline to a continent other than the one on which its owner was planning to play.

triple bogey Three strokes more than par on a hole. Four strokes more than par is a quadruple bogey, 5 more is a quintuple, 6 is a sextuple, 7 is a throwuple, 8 is a blowuple, and 9 is an ohshuttuple.

unplayable ball

The rules of golf make the player "the sole judge" of whether his or her ball is unplayable, and most players use this judicial power to waive the usual penalty for moving the ball in light of their standing in the community.

up & down

up & down

Holing out from off the green in two strokes: an approach shot and a single putt. It is more common for players to go "up, across, beyond, next to, around, and down" or "up, way over, under, into, through, along, onto, beside, and down."

USGA
The United States Golf Association, which is responsible for drafting and enforcing regulations in America. It stands in the same relation to golfers as the Securities and Exchange Commission does to stock manipulators and inside traders.

Vardon grip

The most popular golf grip, in which the little finger of the right hand overlaps the forefinger of the left. Its invention is attributed to the legendary player Harry Vardon, a true innovator in the game who also originated the tradition of professional golfers blaming noises from the gallery for spoiled shots, known as the "Vardon Gripe."

waggle A move employed by many golfers to trigger the swing in which the club is swept back and forth behind or over the ball anywhere from 2 to 500 times.

warm-up drive

An informal, unofficial, orthopedic drive or "medicine ball" deliberately hit sharply left or right, often without prior notice, in an effort to immediately loosen up a suddenly stiff hip or back in order to head off a more serious injury.

warm-up
exercises
Although golf is not as physically demanding as most other sports, it certainly doesn't hurt to loosen up one's muscles before a round. Here are a few simple exercises designed to get you ready for the day's play:

- Hold out your arm, make a fist, and shake it back and forth, then open the fist, palm facing inward, extend the

middle finger, and pump your hand
up and down.

- Kick at the ground, then stomp on it,
  first with your right foot, then with
  your left, then jump up and down.
- Take off your hat, grasp it in your hand,
  throw it on the ground, pick it up,
  and repeat.
- Raise your arms over your head, fists
  clenched, wave them vigorously, and
  let out as loud a scream as you can,
  holding it for at least 10 seconds.

280 | A DUFFER'S DICTIONARY

water hazard

Any boggle ub waddub border
burbled byb reb orb yellob
markglubs stakebles fromble
whidg idg uz legalble, bub
ofteb inadvisabubbble, tub
tryb tub higgle thub ballablub.

water hazard

whiff

Familiar term widely misused to describe a particularly fast and powerful style of practice swing intentionally made directly over the ball.

wind Natural motion of the air. There are four basic winds that golfers generally encounter on a course: a headwind; a wind that blows squarely in their faces; a wind that blows from the green toward the tee; and a wind that blows from a point directly in front of them to a point directly behind them.

winter rules

winter rules
Local rules that permit balls to be lifted, cleaned, and replaced in a more favorable "preferred lie" without penalty during periods when adverse weather conditions make proper maintenance of the fairways impractical. Most golfers generally adhere to winter rules from the first week of November until Halloween.

woods

1. Type of club used to hit a ball a long distance. *2.* Place where the ball lands after being hit a long distance.

wrist In golfers, the swollen joint that connects a sore hand to an aching elbow and a throbbing shoulder.

X-outs
A series of "X's" are printed over the brand name of some golf balls to indicate that, because of some minor imperfections, they are "seconds" and are sold at a deep discount from the price normally charged for the ball. Although they seem very expensive, golf balls are in fact a lot cheaper than they were in the early days of the game, when the handmade, goosedown-stuffed, leather-covered "featherie" or the rubber "guttie"

represented a sizable investment, but it can still be painful to lose one. Thus, golfers who routinely hit errant shots will switch to an X-out ball on a hole with a water hazard, or, if they really lack confidence, a "range ball" (one taken from a driving range), a "smilie" (a ball with a deep cut in it), or a "filchie" (a ball surreptitiously removed from another golfer's bag).

yard One of the basic units of measurement in golf which, when used to report the length of a drive, is 22 inches. Some other measurements players employ include: the stroke (2 swings = 1 stroke); 5 minutes spent looking for a lost ball (1,000 seconds); a 30-foot putt (divide by 5 if preceded by

the phrase "I sunk a" and by
10 if preceded by the phrase
"I missed a"); and the club-length
in determining how far a ball can
be dropped away from a hazard
(the length of the clubhouse
along its longest axis, not including
stairs or porches).

yips Nervous affliction that causes players to miss very short putts which can be cured by using an exaggerated stiff-armed, shoulder-centered putting stroke, or switching to a long-handled putter, or playing exclusively with blind golfers.

zero *1.* A hole-in-none.
A "goose egg" on a hole is
theoretically possible if, in a
rub of the green, an outside
agency, such as an animal,
should snatch the ball off the
tee during a player's backswing,
run with it to the green, and
deposit it in the hole; and if a
player with a handicap greater

than 18 scores a hole-in-one on a par 3 in a tournament, he would have a net "one-for-none" or a "naught." 2. The chances of a golfer who puts down a "0" on a scorecard of ever getting another golf game.

zero

zip code The roughly rectangular area surrounding the tee within which golfers attempt to confine the flight of the ball.

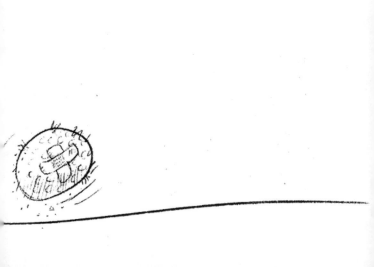